SAXOPHONE

Easy GERSHWIN FOR ALTO SAXOPHONE

Music Department
OXFORD UNIVERSITY PRESS
Oxford and New York

Saxophone in E♭

1. FUNNY FACE
(Funny Face)

2. SUMMERTIME
(Porgy and Bess)

Printed in Great Britain
OXFORD UNIVERSITY PRESS, MUSIC DEPARTMENT, GREAT CLARENDON STREET, OXFORD OX2 6DP

2

3. BEGINNER'S LUCK
(Shall we Dance?)

4. LOVE IS HERE TO STAY
(The Goldwyn Follies)

5. NICE WORK IF YOU CAN GET IT
(A Damsel in Distress)

6. LOVE WALKED IN
(The Goldwyn Follies)

7. I WAS DOING ALL RIGHT
(The Goldwyn Follies)

8. I GOT PLENTY OF NOTHIN'
(Porgy and Bess)

Allegretto

6

9. A FOGGY DAY
(A Damsel in Distress)

10. THEY ALL LAUGHED
(Shall we Dance?)

11. THEY CAN'T TAKE THAT AWAY FROM ME
(Shall we Dance?)

Slowly with warmth

* Traditionally ♪♪♪ is played 𝅘𝅥𝅮₃ 𝅘𝅥𝅮 𝅘𝅥𝅮₃ 𝅘𝅥𝅮

12. LET'S CALL THE WHOLE THING OFF
(Shall we Dance?)

13. IT AIN'T NECESSARILY SO
(Porgy and Bess)

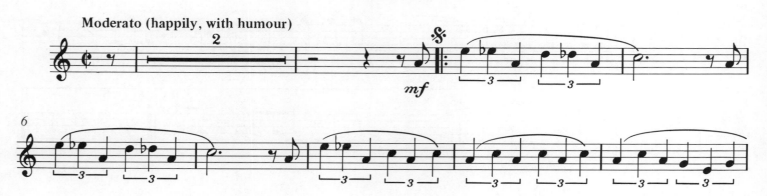

14. I GOT RHYTHM
(Girl Crazy)

Easy GERSHWIN FOR ALTO SAXOPHONE

Fourteen songs
for saxophone and piano

Edited and arranged by
JOHN DAVIES and PAUL HARRIS

Music Department
OXFORD UNIVERSITY PRESS
Oxford and New York

Oxford University Press, Great Clarendon Street, Oxford OX2 6DP, England

Oxford is a trade mark of Oxford University Press

© *Oxford University Press 1989*

This collection of Gershwin songs has been specially arranged for players between about Grade I and Grade V standard. The pieces are set out approximately in order of increasing difficulty—the first few are very easy and playable by a virtual beginner; other notes and more complex rhythms are introduced as progressively as the music will allow. A separate saxophone part is included.

PAUL HARRIS

CONTENTS

1. FUNNY FACE
(Funny Face)

Printed in Great Britain

OXFORD UNIVERSITY PRESS, MUSIC DEPARTMENT, GREAT CLARENDON STREET, OXFORD OX2 6DP

2. SUMMERTIME
(Porgy and Bess)

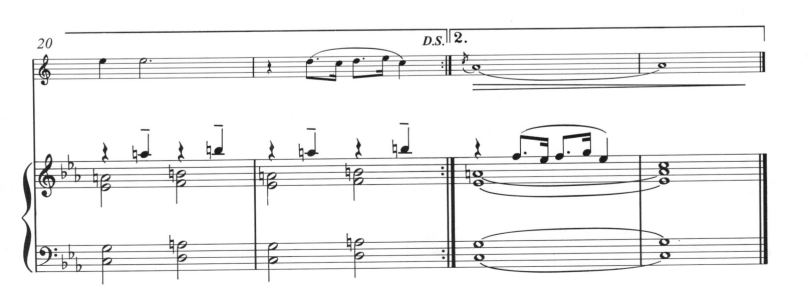

3. BEGINNER'S LUCK

(Shall we Dance?)

4. LOVE IS HERE TO STAY
(The Goldwyn Follies)

5. NICE WORK IF YOU CAN GET IT
(A Damsel in Distress)

Moderato (smoothly)

6. LOVE WALKED IN
(The Goldwyn Follies)

14

7. I WAS DOING ALL RIGHT
(The Goldwyn Follies)

* Where appropriate play as follows: *etc.*

8. I GOT PLENTY OF NOTHIN'
(Porgy and Bess)

9. A FOGGY DAY
(A Damsel in Distress)

Moderato (warmly)

10. THEY ALL LAUGHED
(Shall we Dance?)

Moderato (gracefully and happily)

11. THEY CAN'T TAKE THAT AWAY FROM ME
(Shall we Dance?)

Slowly with warmth

* Traditionally ♪♪♪ is played ♪₃♪ ♪₃♪

12. LET'S CALL THE WHOLE THING OFF

(Shall we Dance?)

13. IT AIN'T NECESSARILY SO

(Porgy and Bess)

28

14. I GOT RHYTHM
(Girl Crazy)

Lively, with abandon

Printed in England by Caligraving Limited Thetford Norfolk